# Mighty Samson

A Three-Act Play

To watch the play, please scan the following QR Code:
Mighty Samson

**Dr. Sultan bin Muhammad Al-Qasimi**

# Mighty Samson

## A Three-Act Play

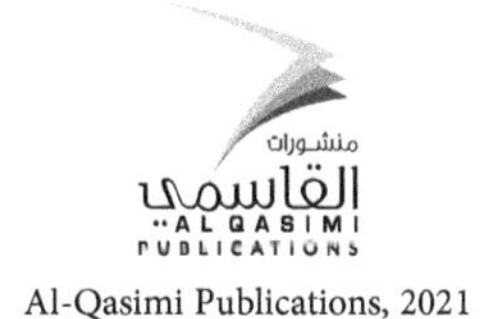


Al-Qasimi Publications, 2021

Book Title: Mighty Samson (A Three-Act Play)
First published in 2008 in Arabic as “Shamshun Al-Jabbar”
by : Al-Qasimi Publications
Author: Dr. Sultan bin Muhammad Al-Qasimi (United Arab Emirates)
Publisher Name: Al-Qasimi Publications
Sharjah, United Arab Emirates
Edition: First
Year of publication: 2021

------------------------------------------
Translated from the Arabic by: Dr. Ahmed Ali
------------------------------
ISBN: 978-9948-469-54-4
Printing Permission: National Media Council, Abu Dhabi, UAE
No. MC 01-03-5337156, Date: 05-08-2021

Age Classification: E
The age group that matches the content of the books was classified according to the age classification issued by the National Council for Media
----------------------------------------------
Al- Qasimi Publications, Al Tarfa, Sheikh Mohammed Bin Zayed Road
PO Box 64009 Sharjah, United Arab Emirates
Tel: 0097165090000, Fax: 0097165520070
Email: info@aqp.ae

# CONTENTS

# Foreword

This play coincides with the $60^{th}$ anniversary of the *Nakbah*. People are still talking as if the conflict between the Palestinians and the Israelis only started 60 years ago. In fact, the conflict dates back to 1122 BC when Palestine was ruled by no one else but the Palestinians themselves. The Israelites were subjects under the Philistines/Palestinians at the time. I wrote this play, Mighty Samson, to highlight this point. I extracted the story and the historical details from the Bible itself.[1]

In the West in general, the word 'philistine' has been used for centuries to refer to an uncultured and barbaric person. In English, the word is used as a derogatory term. This stands in clear contradiction to

1- Bible, Old Testament, Judges 13-16, 1 Samuel 4-6, 1 Samuel 9-31.

the fact that the Philistine (Palestinian) civilization was much superior to that of their enemies, the Israelites, especially in terms of the advancement in applied sciences, war tactics, and fine arts. In modern times, the Israelis and Americans acknowledged this fact.

It is also clear from the archaeological discoveries that the ancient Philistines (Palestinians) had beautifully designed pottery, stylish houses and were well versed in writing in their own language.

Research also show that they enjoyed high level of organization in war. Their forces included cavalry and horse-drawn carriages. They were also very skilled in the manufacturing of metal tools.[1]

The Bible states in 1 Samuel 13:19-20 "Not a blacksmith could be found in the whole land of Israel. So whenever the Israelites needed to sharpen their plowshares, picks, axes, or sickles, they had to take them to a Philistine blacksmith."

The Bible clearly insinuates that the Philistines (Palestinians) were guilty of not sharing their technical skills with the Israelites. It is terribly disheartening to see that the cause of the Biblical prejudice against

---

1- a- Donald Ryan (an archaeologist), (World of the Bible), Alpha Books 2003.
b- A. Raban and R.R Stieglitz, (the Sea Peoples and their Contributions to Civilisation) in British Archaeological Reports : 17, 1991,6, pp. 34-42, 91-2.
c- Frank Moore Cross and Lawrence E. Stager, The Israel Exploration Journal, 2007.
(They were part of the `Harvard University archaeological project in Ashkelon).

the Philistines (Palestinians) was because the writers of the Bible were in war against the Philistines. Such enmity managed to find its way to the western nations and the Jews alike. The result has been the antagonistic stand against the Palestinians that we are still witnessing to the present day.

Would the Palestinians ever find justice?

# Cast of Characters

According to Appearance

- Some Jews
- First Jew
- Second Jew
- Samson
- Third Jew
- A group of Jews
- A group of Philistines
- Delilah
- Philistines' Rulers
- 1st Ruler
- 2nd Ruler
- 3rd Ruler

- Barber
- A Companion of Philistines' Rulers
- A second group of Philistines
- Executioner
- A philistine
- A second group of Philistines
- A boy
- A Hajib
- Gaza Representative
- A group of Jews
- Samuel, the Judge
- A Jewish Attendee
- Guard
- King Saul
- Israelite soldiers
- Philistine soldiers
- Jonathan
- Abinadab
- Malki-Shua
- 1st Philistine Warrior
- 2nd Philistine Warrior
- 2nd Philistine Warrior

- Armor-Bearer of King Saul
- 1st Philistine
- 2nd Philistine
- 3rd Philistine
- Philistines' Leader

# Act I

## Scene One

**Place:** The Rock of Etam, to the west of Beir Zeit, where Samson, the son of Manoah, of the Dan tribe of the town of Zorah is hiding in a cave.

**Time:** 1122 BCE

*Some Jews from Juda, between the Dead Sea and the Mediterranean Sea, enter. One of them shouts:*

**1st Jew:** Samson, Samson!

*Samson comes out from the cave.*

**2nd Jew:** The Philistines have attacked us. When we asked them why, they said they had come to arrest you. And when we asked them why again, they said they wanted to avenge what you had done to the Philistines. We, the men of Juda, all 3000 have come to say to you: Don't you realize that the Philistines are rulers over us? What have you done to us?

**Samson:** I merely did to them what they did to me.

**3rd Jew:** What did they do to you?

**Samson:** A while ago, I went to Temnah (*between Ramallah and Lydda*). There, I saw a young Philistine woman whose beauty captured me. So, when I returned home I asked my parents to let me marry her. But they refused and said "Isn't there an acceptable woman among your relatives or among all our Hebrew people? Why marry a Philistine?" But when I insisted, they approved and I went down to Temna with my father and mother. On the way, a lion came roaring toward me. I grabbed it and ripped it apart with my bare hands. I was certain that the spirit of God moved upon me, divinely empowering me. In Temna, the girl's father agreed to our marriage and allowed me to sit with her. My heart was filled with happiness as I talked with her. When I went to Ashkelon, the Lord empowered me again and I struck down 30 Philistines and went home with everything they had.

**1st Jew:** Then what?

**Samson:** Then, at the time of wheat harvest, I took a young goat and went to visit my wife. But her father would not let me go in to see her and said I came too late, and that he married her off to one of my companions. And he wanted me to marry her sister instead saying she was more attractive. So, I said to her father "This time I have a right to get even with the Philistines; I will really harm them"

**2nd Jew:** The philistines say you burnt their wheat fields and destroyed their olive groves and vineyards. Did you do so?

**Samson:** Yes, I did; because my wife's father married her off to one of my men. When the Philistines found out that one of them gave his daughter in marriage to a Jew, they went up and burned her and her father to death. So, I swore I won't stop until I get my revenge on you, Philistines. I attacked them viciously and slaughtered many of them. Then I went down and stayed in this cave in the rock of Etam.

**3rd Jew:** Well, We've come to tie you up and hand you over to the Philistines.

**Samson:** I agree, provided that you swear to me that you won't kill me yourselves.

**1st Jew:** Agreed, We will only tie you up and hand you over to them. We will not kill you

*The Jews bring some ropes and bind his arms behind his back; then tie the ropes round him.*

**2nd Jew:** Let's go to hand him over to the Philistines in Lahi (near Gaza).

**Darkness.**

## Scene Two

**Place:** The village of Lahi, near Gaza.

*A crowd of Philistines come to arrest Samson.*

**3rd Jew:** O, Philistines! Come over to take Samson!

*The Philistines come toward them shouting … They get hold of Samson who fights back. He tenses his muscles and arms and the ropes are torn and the bindings drop from his hands. The Philistines gather round him in an attempt to capture him.*

*He finds a fresh jawbone of a donkey. So, he grabs it and fights them with it. He strikes down a thousand men.*

*He stands up proudly and raises his arms with the fresh jawbone of the donkey*

**Samson:** With the jawbone of a donkey, I've made heaps of them. With the jawbone of a donkey I've killed a thousand men.

*Samson throws away the jawbone of the donkey, raises his arms up to the Heaven and shouts:*

**Samson:** My Lord, You have given your servant this great victory. Must I now die of thirst and fall into the hands of the Philistines?

*The Lord answers his prayer and water gushes from the ground.*

**Samson** (*shouting*): Water! Water! O, My Lord! The water is gushing from the ground.

*Samson drinks. His strength returns and he is revived.*

**Samson:** I will call this water spring "*En Hakkore, caller's spring*". I will be the Leader of all the Jewish tribes and their Judge.

# Act II

## Scene One

**Setting:** House of Delilah, the Jewess

**Place:** The Valley of Sorek, 15 miles west of Zorah, under Philistines' rule.

**Time:** 1105 BCE

*To one side of the stage appears a door to an inner room wherein Delilah, worried, walks about looking right and left as if in wait for someone. Knocking on the door is heard.*

**Delilah:** Who's at the door?

**Philistines' Rulers:** It is us, the Rulers of Palestine. Open up.

*Delilah opens the door. Three men carrying their*

*bows and arrows come in together with a guard carrying a spear.*

**1st Ruler** (*pointing at his company*): We, the Rulers of Palestine, had asked you to lure him into showing you the secret of his great strength and how we can overpower him so we may tie him up and subdue him. But you did not.

**2nd Ruler:** We know he's in love with you, and we do not think he will hide his secret from you. So, if you succeed each one of us will give you eleven hundred shekels of silver, as promised.

**Delilah:** I asked him three times; the first he said to me "If anyone ties me with seven fresh bowstrings that have not been dried, I'll become as weak as any other man." So, I tied him, but as soon as I called to him (Samson, the Philistines are upon you!), he snapped the bowstrings as easily as a piece of string snaps when it comes close to a flame. The second time I tied him securely with new ropes that have never been used, as he told me. But he snapped the ropes off his arms as if they were threads. The third time, he said to me "If you weave the seven braids of my head into the fabric on the loom and tighten it with the pin, I'll become as weak as any other man". So, I did, and when I shouted

(Samson, the Philistines are upon you!), he awoke from his sleep and pulled up the pin and the loom, with the fabric.

**3rd Ruler:** Well, you've sent for us to come again now. Is anything the matter?

**1st Ruler:** Have you uncovered the secret of his great strength?

**Delilah:** Yes, he told me everything. But have you brought the money?

*Each Ruler of the Philistines brings forth a money sack to show her.*

**Delilah:** Wait outside till I call you.

*The Rulers of the Philistines leave the house.*

*Samson comes out from the inner room while Delilah is sitting in the house court.*

**Samson:** Delilah! Who's with you?

**Delilah:** No one. Come over here my love, and sleep on my lap.

**Delilah** (*nagging Samson*): How can you say, 'I love you,' when you won't confide in me? Three times you have made a fool of me and haven't told me the secret of your great strength.

**Samson:** You have nagged me every night with the same question "What's the secret of your strength? What's the secret of your strength?" I am sick to death of it. In spite of this I did confess to you the secret of my strength and said "If the seven braids of my head were shaved, my strength would leave me, and I would become as weak as any other man."

**Delilah:** Is that so?

**Samson:** Yes.

**Delilah:** Sleep my love! Sleep on my lap.

*Samson is sound asleep. Delilah puts his head down and leaves.*

*Then she returns with a barber holding a big pair of scissors and gets closer to Samson's head. The barber shaves off the seven braids of Samson's hair, then runs out quickly.*

*Delilah sits back next to Samson.*

**Delilah** (*screaming*): Samson, the Philistines are upon you!

*Samson rises and tries to show his strength, but in vain. He falls to his knees. Delilah jumps over him and overpowers him. She realizes his strength truly left him. So, she shouts:*

**Delilah** (*shouting*): O, Philistines! O, Philistines! Come! Come!

*The three Philistine Rulers and the escort with the spear come in and seize him. Delilah rushes into the inner room and returns with chains and shackles. The Rulers of the Philistines bind him securely and drag him to the front of the stage. They throw Delilah the money sacks, then gouge out Samson's eyes and throw them right and left on the stage. Samon's eyes bleed as he screams in agony and humiliation.*

**Samson:** Arrrrrrrrgh! Arrrrrrrrgh!

**Philistine Ruler:** Let's take him to Gaza.

*Samson is dragged in his shackles and stumbles as he walks out of the stage.*

*Delilah returns with Samson's braids of hair in one hand and the scissors in the other. She shrieks and looks disturbed as to what happened to Samson. But, she soon throws away the hair and the scissors; gazes at the money and laughs with joy.*

## Scene Two

*The Philistines celebrate their victory over Samson.*

**Place:** Gaza

**Time:** 1105 BCE

**Setting:** The Rulers of the Philistines sitting with the crowds, around 3000 men and women, in the temple. In the middle are two pillars that support the temple roof. To one side of the stage, Samson is seen grinding grain in the Prison. Behind him is a guard whipping him.

*The festival begins with Philistine dances and acrobatic show.*

**A Philistine:** Our God has granted us victory over Samson.

**A group of Philistines:** Praise be our God who has

delivered our enemy into our hands, the one who laid waste our land and multiplied our slain.

**A Philistine Ruler:** Bring Samson out of the prison.

*A boy leads Samson, with his hair long, out of prison. The boy stands him between the two pillars that support the ceiling of the temple.*

**Usher:** Fellowmen! Here is Samson, the son of Manoah, from the town of Zorah, Judge of the Jewish tribes for 20 years; now under Philistines' rule.

**A Philistine Ruler:** All the judges have been under Philistine rule except for you, Samson. You attacked people, killed them, burnt their crops and violated their honour.

**A Philistine Ruler:** We have a complaint from the people of Gaza.

*The Ruler turns and asks about the representative of the Gaza people.*

**A Philistine Ruler:** Where is the Gaza representative?

*A man comes forward.*

**A Philistine Ruler:** What is your complaint?

**Gaza Representative:** One day, Samson came to Gaza where he went in to a prostitute's house and spent the night with her. The news spread that Samson was there. The people of Gaza gathered and lay in wait for him all night at the closed city gate intending to kill him at dawn. But Samson lay there only until the middle of the night. Then he got up and took hold of the doors of the city gate, together with the two posts, and tore them loose, bar and all. He lifted them to his shoulders and carried them to the top of the hill that faces Hebron.

**A Philistine Ruler:** Then?

**Gaza Representative:** Samson is a libertine who violated many women. He must be killed.

**A Philistine Ruler:** We had ruled before that Samson was to be bound with bronze shackles and to be set to grind grain in prison. He has already spent a period of time there. Now, we rule that he dances to entertain us. Come on!

*The Philistines start to clap and ask Samson to dance for them.*

**A group of Philistines:** Samson, dance! Dance! Dance! Dance!

*Samson begins to jump pretending to dance. He talk to the boy who held his hand into the temple.*

**Samson:** My boy, put my hands where I can feel the pillars that support the temple, so that I may lean against them.

*The boy leads him to the first pillar then to the second. Samson stands where his hands touch both pillars at the same time. As the dancing and clapping goes on, Samson shouts at the top of his voice:*

**Samson:** Sovereign LORD. Please, God, strengthen me just once more, and let me with one blow get revenge on the Philistines for my two eyes.

*Samson pushes the pillars with all his might as he screams:*

**Samson:** My Lord, let me die with the Philistines.

*Down comes the temple on Samson and all the Philistines in it.*

*Samson is killed together with thousands of Philistines as the temple collapses on them. A Thick cloud of dust.*

**A philistine** (*seeing the dust shouts*): There were 3000 men and women, and the Rulers of the Philistines, and Samson himself. O, my God! O, my God! This is a disaster!

# Act III

## Scene One

*Saul is crowned first King of the Kingdom of Israel.*

**Place:** Village of Shakhem, near Naples

**Time:** 1050 BCE

**Setting:** A crowd of people shouting and arguing.

*Samuel, the Judge, walks in. The arguing and the shouting stop.*

*Samuel goes toward one side of the stage.*

**Attendant:** O, Judge. You have been for us the one in charge of the Jewish tribes; and you used to warn us that if we were to set up a King upon us we would suffer from the dealings of the king. So, why are you here today?

**Samuel:** I came to crown Saul as the first King of the Kingdom of Israel.

**All** (*in one voice*): Why?

**Samuel:** You know that Samson had killed a great number of the Philistines. And, when he destroyed the temple, 3000 more were killed, that is, many more when he died than while he lived. I said to myself then that the Philistines would never recover from that disaster.And now for 55 years after Samson's death, many judges have ruled over you, and I am the last of them. We only have military command, while politics have always been in the hands of the Tribal Chiefs of the Jews. The Israelites have degenerated into a life of chaos: no worship of God, and everyone does as one likes. But for the Philistines to attack out temple and seize the Ark of the Covenant and the tablets, this is unacceptable. I am your Judge, but I've grown old and I cannot fight to get the Ark of the Covenant back. So, I thought if Saul is made King, he could bring back the Ark of the Covenant.

*Someone knocks the door. A guard opens the door and is given a box, which he brings into the meeting hall. When all see it, they cheer loudly.*

**All:** The Ark of the Covenant! The Ark of the Covenant!

**Attendant:** Open it to see; they might have broken the tablets!

*The box is handed in to Samuel who opens it and takes the commandments' tablet in one piece. Everyone sighs in relief and joy.*

**All:** Praise be the Lord!

**Samuel** (*to the Guard*): Guard, why did you let the man who delivered the tablets go?

**Guard:** When he handed it in to me he said "Take your Ark of the Covenant"; it has brought us nothing but bad fortune". I was so happy that I took it and rushed with it to bring it in.

**Attendant:** Judge, since making Saul King was to bring back the Ark of the Covenant, what is the need now, that we have retrieved it, to make Saul king?

**Samuel:** It is to be done!

*Samuel looks at one side of the stage and says:*

**Samuel:** Here is King Saul coming ...

*Saul enters dressed in the King's attire. A person enters carrying a crown. All rise to greet King Saul.*

*Saul sits on the throne. Samuel comes forward to crown Saul while sitting on the throne, then he retreats to his previous position.*

**King Saul:** I am the King ... and I shall call my kingdom, the Kingdom of Israel, with me as its first sovereign, and this village, Shekhem as its capital, where we will celebrate.

*Judge Samuel carries the Ark of the Covenant and presents it to King Saul to show him the Commandments' tablet.*

**Saul** (*surprised and joyous*): Who brought it back?

**Samuel:** They themselves did.

**Saul:** Why? Were they scared that we may retrieve it by force?

**Samuel:** They returned it because it brought them bad fortune.

**Saul:** We will be their worst fortune! Those barbarians!

**Samuel:** The Philistines have made new alliances with the Ammonites to the East and with the Amalekites to the South.

**Saul:** Fear not, I will fight the Ammonites and the Amalekites and destroy them.

## Scene Two

*Battlefield with the Philistines*

**Place:** Mount Gilboa, near Jenin

**Time:** 1010 BCE

*King Saul addresses the Israelite soldiers.*

**King Saul:** Soldiers, these Philistines have come to fight us. They want to destroy our state. Do you remember when I fought the Ammonites and destroyed them so completely that they could not rise again? And do you remember when I fought the Amalekites and destroyed them so completely that they could not rise again? Today, with you beside me, I fight the Philistines and they have no onc on their side. And as such, we must defeat them.

*The Israelites line up in one side of the stage and the Philistines in the other.*

*King Saul of the Israelites comes forward and says:*

**King Saul:** I am King Saul, first King of Israel. You've heard about me when I destroyed the Ammonites and the Amalekites. Are there warriors amongst you who can challenge each of my three sons, Jonathan, Abinadab and Malki-Shua, to a duel?

*A Philistine warrior steps forward.*

**Saul:** Go forth, Jonathan!

*Jonathan goes forward and a duel ensues. Jonathan Son of King Saul gets killed. Two Israelite soldiers go to pull Jonathan's corpse to the side of the Israelites'. The Philistine warrior goes back to join his side.*

**Saul:** Here is my son, Abinadab. Go forth, Abinadab!

*Abinadab goes forward and a Philistine warrior comes out to fight him. A duel follows Abinadab gets killed. Two Israelite soldiers go to pull Abinadab's corpse to the side of the Israelites'. The Philistine warrior goes back to join his side.*

**Saul:** Here is my son, Malki-Shua. Go forth, Malki-Shua!

*Malki-Shua goes forward and a third Philistine warrior comes out to fight him. A duel follows Malki-Shua gets killed. Two Israelite soldiers go to pull Malki-Shua's corpse to the side of the Israelites'. The Philistine warrior goes back to join his side.*

*When Saul sees his three sons killed, he shouts to his army:*

**Saul:** O, Israelites, Kill the Philistines! Kill the Philistines! Kill the Philistines!

*The Israelites march to the middle of the stage and they are bombarded with arrows. King Saul is injured by many arrows. He calls his armor-bearer:*

**Saul:** Armor-bearer! Armor-bearer!

*A man comes forward carrying the King's arms.*

**Armor-Bearer:** Yes, my King!

**Saul:** Draw your sword and run me through.

*The armor-bearer steps backward in shock at what he was told and shakes his head 'No'.*

**Saul:** Draw your sword and run me through, or these Philistine fellows will come and run me through and abuse me.

*The armor-bearer walks round the king and keeps saying:*

**Armor-Bearer:** No! No! No!

*Saul takes his own sword and falls on it. The sword penetrates his body. He falls dead on the ground. The armour-bearer screams and cries in shock. When he sees that Saul is dead, he too falls on his sword and dies with him.*

*A moment of silence followed by the fall of darkness indicating a night has passed since the battle started.*

*A noise is heard from a distance. It gets closer. The Philistines reach the stage. They march forward and gather the Israelites' arms scattered all over and among the dead.*

*A Philistine recognizes the three sons of King Saul.*

**A Philistine:** Here are the sons of King Saul. The three are dead!

**2nd Philistine:** Here is King Saul himself, dead!

**3rd Philistine:** Cut off his head!

*The 2nd Philistine cuts off King Saul's head and raises it on the top of his spear for all to see. The philistines cheer!*

**The Philistines:** We won! We won!

*In the meantime, the Philistines' leader comes forward.*

**Philistines' Leader:** Yesterday, we killed Saul and his three sons and all his men. Do not think that the war is over. We still need to liberate all our towns from the Israelites. We must start now.

*The Philistines cheer louder. A Philistine rushes into the stage shouting:*

**The Philistine:** O, Philistines! O, Philistines! When the news about the death of King Saul, his three sons and all his men reached the towns and the Israelites heard it, they abandoned their towns and fled. And the Philistines came and took over them.

*Everyone is overcome with joy and all join in typical Philistine singing and dancing.*

www.ingramcontent.com/pod-product-compliance
Ingram Content Group UK Ltd.
Pitfield, Milton Keynes, MK11 3LW, UK
UKHW021958190726
13853UKWH00004B/1610

9 789948 469544